SO-BFE-499

DIGGING UP THE PAST

POMPEII
CITY OF ASHES

Sarah Pitt Kaplan

HIGH
interest
books

Children's Press®
A Division of Scholastic Inc.
New York / Toronto / London / Auckland / Sydney
Mexico City / New Delhi / Hong Kong
Danbury, Connecticut

Book Design: Chris Logan and Jennifer Crilly
Contributing Editors: Matt Pitt and Kevin Somers
Photo Credits: Cover, pp. 1, 25 © Roger Ressmeyer/Corbis; p. 4 © E. O. Hoppé/Corbis; pp. 6–7 © The State Russian Museum/Corbis; p. 8 © 2002 Geoatlas; pp. 11, 36 © O. Louis Mazzatenta/ National Geographic Image Collection; p.13 Illustration by Jennifer Crilly; p. 15 © Mimmo Jodice/Corbis; p. 16 © Corbis; p. 19 © Getty Images; p. 21 © Richard T. Nowitz/Corbis; p. 23 © Bettmann/Corbis; pp. 26, 31 © The Art Archive/Dagli Orti; p. 33 Archivo Iconografico, S.A./Corbis; p. 35 © Araldo de Luca/Corbis; p. 40 © Jonathan Blair/Corbis

Library of Congress Cataloging-in-Publication Data

Kaplan, Sarah Pitt.
    Pompeii : city of ashes / Sarah Pitt Kaplan.
    p. cm. — (Digging up the past)
    Includes bibliographical references and index.
    ISBN 0-516-25122-8 (lib. bdg.) — ISBN 0-516-25091-4 (pbk.)
    1. Pompeii (Extinct city)—Juvenile literature. 2. Vesuvius (Italy)—Eruption, 79—Juvenile literature. 3. Excavations (Archaeology)—Italy—Pompeii (Extinct city)—Juvenile literature. I. Title. II. Digging up the past (Children's Press)

    DG70.P7K37 2005
    937'.7—dc22
                                            2004026653

3 4 5 6 7 8 9 10 R 14 13 12 11 10 09 08

CONTENTS

This photo from the 1930s shows the ruins of Pompeii. In the background, a smoking Mount Vesuvius reminds us of its awesome power.

Introduction

It is a sunny day in Italy in 1594. A man named Domenico Fontana is digging a ditch. He is building an irrigation trench. As he digs, he uncovers something very important. Fontana finds a marble wall with writing on it. The wall is a remainder of an ancient city that was destroyed centuries before. Amazingly, Fontana has begun to uncover the lost city of Pompeii (Pom-**pay**).

On an August day in A.D. 79, the ground of Pompeii rumbled and quaked. A sleeping volcano overlooking the city had awoken. On this day, Mount Vesuvius erupted. Darkness covered the sky. People living hundreds of miles away felt the raging eruption. Hot black ash rained down on Pompeii. Many people choked to death on fumes. Others were buried under 12 feet (3.7 meters) of ash.

In a matter of hours, a flourishing city became a ghost town. The town remained untouched for centuries. Grass and flowers grew over its volcanic tomb. But the debris that buried Pompeii also preserved it. Mount Vesuvius may have destroyed Pompeii, but it also froze the city in time. Because of this, scientists have been able to uncover many of the city's wondrous treasures.

The deadly eruption of Mount Vesuvius has become an important tool to help us unlock the mysteries of ancient Roman life.

In 1833, artist Karl Pavlovic Briullov painted his vision of what the tragedy at Pompeii might have been like. The painting is entitled *The Last Day of Pompeii*.

North Sea

EUROPE

Italy

● Rome

● Herculaneum
● Pompeii

Mediterranean Sea

AFRICA

The ruins of Pompeii are located south of Rome on the western coast of Italy.

CHAPTER ONE

Victims of Vesuvius

Before the Blast

P ompeii was an ancient city on the coast of Italy. It was founded in the seventh century B.C. by a tribe called the Oscans. Over the years, many tribes settled in the area. Many empires tried to rule Pompeii. In 80 B.C. Pompeii became a Roman colony.

Pompeii thrived as a Roman colony. The people were eager to work, and the soil was perfect for growing grapes and olives. Roman art and architecture appeared throughout the seaside city.

Then, in A.D. 62, disaster struck when an earthquake rocked Pompeii. The impact of this disaster was enormous. Homes and roads were destroyed. The city's water supply was ruined. Yet with Roman help, the city was rebuilt. Over the next seventeen years, workers restored wrecked buildings. Ruined artwork was replaced. Restaurants and shops were built and began to thrive. The population of the city soared to over twenty thousand. Even wealthy Romans came to Pompeii to spend their vacations.

However, in August A.D. 79, things suddenly changed. Around noon on a warm day, Mount Vesuvius blew its top. Dust and ash shot out of the mountain's cone. Showers of debris blackened the sky. This debris landed on the city, covering its streets. Wind blew ash into open windows of homes and businesses. Small rocks battered rooftops, causing them to collapse. Within hours, cinder and dust coated nearly every inch of Pompeii.

Pompeii's citizens were shocked. They thought Vesuvius was an extinct volcano. After all, it had been inactive for three hundred years! They believed the volcano would never erupt again.

The panic in the city grew with each hour. Children shrieked helplessly. Everyone pushed through the debris, scrambling for cover. People could barely see in front of them because of the clouds of hot, burning ash. Nearly blinded by the thick clouds, people screamed out their loved ones' names, hoping a familiar voice would respond.

The tragedy of Mount Vesuvius destroyed many lives, but it preserved priceless treasures. These gold snake bracelets and earrings were found next to the body of a woman.

Many fled the city, escaping with their lives. Those who stayed behind weren't so lucky. Some were crushed by falling debris. Others were trampled to death.

Many people darted home to gather their valuables. Some stole the valuables left behind by those who had fled Pompeii. Many of these thieves paid dearly for their greed. They choked to death on toxic fumes. They suffocated, and were soon buried under heaps of cinder.

Pompeii wasn't the only town caught in the fury of Vesuvius that day. Herculaneum, a nearby town, was also destroyed. A river of boiling mud had flowed down the volcano's side. Within four minutes, the scorching mud washed over Herculaneum.

PRESSURE COOKER

Pompeii's rich farmland came from a deadly source—hardened volcanic ash from Mount Vesuvius. Mount Vesuvius is a stratovolcano. This means it contains alternating layers of ash, cinders, and lava. Stratovolcanoes are topped with a cone-shaped point. Inside this cone, magma and gases slowly churn. Over time, this thick mixture gets caught in the volcano's main vent. The pressure inside the volcano grows. Finally, it explodes with the force of a nuclear bomb.

Evidence of the Eruption

For centuries, most of our information about this disaster came from two letters. A man named Pliny the Younger wrote the letters. He saw Vesuvius erupt while staying with his uncle, Pliny the Elder. He watched from a safe distance, across the Bay of Naples. After a few moments, he alerted his uncle. Pliny the Elder commanded a Roman fleet near Pompeii. After the eruption, he set out for Pompeii.

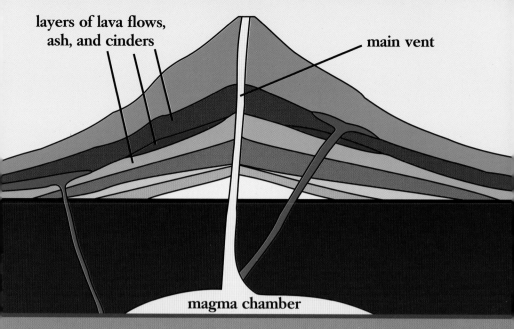

layers of lava flows, ash, and cinders

main vent

magma chamber

This cross-section of a stratovolcano shows how the many layers of lava, ash, cinders, and other volcanic rock build up to form a steep cone-shaped volcano.

At first, he went out of curiosity. As he came closer to Vesuvius, Pliny the Elder saw how the victims were suffering. His curiosity turned to terror. He launched a rescue mission to save his countrymen. However, the sea's crashing waves were too brutal. His boats couldn't reach the shore. Frustrated, he sailed to a neighboring town. He planned to restart his rescue mission the next morning.

But Pliny the Elder never saw another dawn. That night, the gusts of toxic gas that Vesuvius belched out grew deadlier. Anyone unlucky enough to breathe in the toxins died. This included Pliny the Elder. He failed to rescue Pompeii's victims. Worse, he had become a victim, too. His nephew wrote his letters as a tribute to his uncle. Pliny the Younger wanted the world to know about his uncle's sacrifice. However, his letters did much more. They helped historians piece together the events of that fateful night.

ARTIFACT

Pliny the Younger's letters were recovered nearly fifteen hundred years after he wrote them!

The accounts of the eruption describe unspeakable horrors. Pliny the Younger wrote about seeing a towering cloud rise over Vesuvius. It was shaped like a mushroom. The cloud shot steam and bits of lava into the sky. He described watching "great tongues of fire" lift over the volcano. Later, he saw "the sea sucked away . . . from the shore." This happened because the sea had been forced back by the trembling earth. Soon, "Sea creatures were left stranded on dry sand."

Treasures such as these silver food containers were protected for centuries by the ash that covered Pompeii.

The eruption destroyed the region in a matter of two days. In Pompeii alone, the eruption claimed over two thousand lives. Layers of rock and ash buried the town. But because Pompeii was covered, it was protected from harm. Its treasures were harder for thieves to loot. Pompeii was even protected from weather damage. Pompeii rested under the ash, unharmed, for centuries.

In 1748, King Charles III of Spain began excavating Pompeii's ashy ruins. Many people believe these early digs of Pompeii brought about the science of archaeology.

CHAPTER TWO

Raising the Dead

In the Trenches

Until Fontana's amazing discovery in 1594, Pompeii's secrets had remained hidden for fifteen hundred years. Eventually, Fontana finished digging his irrigation trench. But once he did, no immediate exploration of the buried city was carried out.

Finally, in 1748, King Charles III of Spain took an interest in excavating, or digging up, Pompeii. The king wasn't interested in learning how ancient Romans had lived, though. He was thirsty for wealth, not knowledge. King Charles guessed that many treasures lay beneath the ash. He wanted to decorate his royal court with them. Charles started new excavations near Fontana's trench.

First, excavators towed away tons of lapilli. Lapilli are stony or glassy fragments of lava that are blown out of a volcano's eruption. After finishing this task, Charles's men looted Pompeii. They robbed the site of much of its sculpture and paintings. Those artifacts that were thought worthy of the king's collection were kept. But much of the other ancient art was destroyed.

ARTIFACT

Once the treasures were taken, diggers actually reburied several of Pompeii's buildings.

Despite the careless nature of these early excavations, they were important digs. In fact, some historians claim that the science of archaeology was born at this time. Archaeology is a method of learning about the past by digging up old buildings and objects. Archaeologists then carefully study their findings.

A Lighter Touch

The early digs at Pompeii were anything but careful. When workers uncovered a valuable antique, they didn't record where they had found it. They left behind only sketchy plans of their work. This reckless attitude outraged many people interested in learning more about Rome's ancient past.

Since the middle of the eighteenth century, many different teams of archaeologists have studied the sites of Pompeii and Herculaneum. This photograph is of a Herculaneum dig from around 1929.

Angry protests forced King Charles to rethink his plan. In 1765, he hired a new head archaeologist. Francesco la Vega was put in charge of the Pompeii site. Right away, improvements were made. Under la Vega, better methods of digging were practiced. He ordered that any earth dug up be carried away. This would help clear space for future excavations of the site. He uncovered entire buildings, not just small parts of them. La Vega also kept detailed diaries of his work.

Many people interested in the ancient world began coming to the site. Scholars came to study artifacts. Artists painted watercolors of Pompeii's newfound ruins. Excitement was in the air, and archaeologists were amazed with the discoveries at Pompeii. The entire city seemed to have been frozen in time. Tables were discovered that were fully set for midday meals. These meals, of course, were never eaten. The uncovered city gave visitors a window into everyday Roman life. What did ancient Romans eat and drink? What kinds of clothing did they wear? How did they make money? What did they do for fun?

WRITING HISTORY

Archaeologists found writings preserved in the ruins at Pompeii. This discovery delighted them. They excavated many important items. These included several plaques found next to statues of people. The plaques let historians know about the subject of each statue. Reading the plaques taught archaeologists which citizens were the most admired in Pompeii.

Foods such as these olives were found in the ruins of Pompeii. Items of this type give historians a better idea of what daily life was like in ancient Italy.

Fiorelli's Great Find

From 1863 to 1875, archaeologist Giuseppe Fiorelli excavated Pompeii. His approach to the work was extremely careful and more scientific than earlier digs. He didn't just dig at random, take what he found, and then move on. Fiorelli fully excavated one area at a time. After he completed digging one area, he simply moved to the area next to it. This gave historians a clearer vision of the city's entire layout.

Fiorelli also dug from the top of the buried city to its bottom. His digs began on rooftops. Excavators then worked their way down. This helped them recover more objects. It also allowed them to better preserve the ancient buildings.

Tragic Casts

One of Fiorelli's most important contributions was his invention of plaster casts of body cavities. After suffocating, Pompeii's victims were totally coated in volcanic ash. Because the ash was so hot, the layers clung to the victims' skin like cobwebs. It also bonded to each victim's clothing and jewelry. It even bonded to their facial expressions. As the ash cooled, it hardened. Victims were soon enclosed in an ash cocoon. Over time, the bodies slowly decomposed. Only the hard ash shells remained.

The hollow parts of each ash cocoon were still shaped in the forms of the dead people. Fiorelli injected plaster into the shells. Using this plaster, Fiorelli recreated the final poses of the dead.

The casts are haunting study guides. They tell us what Pompeii's victims were doing during their last moments. One cast captures a frightened dog. The dog was still chained in his master's house when

This plaster cast of a person was made from one of the hardened ash shells that was dug out of Pompeii's ruins. This victim of the Mount Vesuvius disaster was found in this huddled position.

Vesuvius erupted. Other casts uncovered failed rescue missions. One scene shows a man using his body to protect a pregnant woman from debris. Thanks to Fiorelli, this ancient man's heroism has been captured forever.

Fiorelli's body casts have answered many mysteries. By studying them, archaeologists get clues about the victims' backgrounds. One shows a young woman trying to shield a baby from hot ash. Archaeologists noticed the baby was wearing a lot of jewelry. This proves the child came from a wealthy family. The woman, however, wasn't wearing any jewels. She was probably a household servant. There's a good chance she was the infant's nanny. Yet she was willing to give her life to protect the child's.

In this plaster casting, we see a victim of Mount Vesuvius trying to help another person as ash and stone debris rained down on Pompeii.

This courtyard is one of many structures unearthed by the scientists who have studied Pompeii.

CHAPTER THREE

Layout of a Lost City

The eruption of Mount Vesuvius locked Pompeii in an ancient time capsule. Ash kept the city's treasures safe from the ravages of weather and looters. Because of this, archaeologists can observe the entire city's true layout. They have unearthed amazing structures. Many are still in good condition. In some ways, this is thanks to another disaster. As mentioned earlier, an earthquake in A.D. 62 battered Pompeii. Countless buildings were ruined. You will recall that after that eruption, Romans repaired many of the structures.

Writing on the Wall

One repaired building was the Basilica. This was a huge meeting place in Pompeii. Here, people recorded business dealings. The building also contained courts of law. The Basilica is so well preserved that experts have even spotted ancient graffiti on its walls! The graffiti includes wisecracks

This piece of graffiti is a campaign poster for an ancient Roman political election.

and insults. In graffiti, citizens express love for one another. Archaeologists found one piece of graffiti that told the date that it was written. Based on this note, experts concluded that the original Basilica was built late in the second century B.C.

Riot Act

Many other public buildings were found. These include temples and theaters. Archaeologists also found the site where Pompeii's citizens went to watch sports. This building is called an amphitheater. Pompeii's amphitheater was much like today's sports arenas. Instead of watching baseball or soccer, though, these fans enjoyed the fierce games of gladiators.

Ancient Romans shared as much passion for sports as today's fans. There were great rivalries. People cheered for their favorite participants. They screamed and booed others.

Their excitement, however, could get out of hand. That's what happened during a sporting event in A.D. 59. A fight broke out between Pompeii and their opponent. Insults led to throwing punches and stones. Several fans were killed in the brawl.

The amphitheater was actually designed with crowd control in mind. It was built in the city's southeastern corner. The location was far from the town center. This protected peoples' homes from riots. The amphitheater was also near two gates. These gates led people away from Pompeii. If fans were violent, they could get tossed from the city!

ARTIFACT

The deadly riot in Pompeii did not please the Roman emperor Nero. He shut down the amphitheater for ten years!

Wealth of Water

Pompeii was built on a mountain slope. This made it difficult to keep a supply of water. Archaeologists have learned how Pompeii's citizens managed a water supply. In the first century A.D., Pompeii solved its water problem by building *impluvia*, or water tanks. Later, Emperor Augustus built a system of aqueducts, including one in Pompeii. This aqueduct delivered a constant flow of water to the residents of Pompeii.

The people of Pompeii often cleaned themselves in water fountains called bathhouses. They also used public bathrooms. Here, the flow of fresh water kept human waste from building up.

Art Lessons

Diggers at Pompeii have done more than unearth huge buildings. They've also discovered beautiful homes. Many of the objects kept in these homes are still intact. Archaeologists have found glass bottles, furniture, and even baked bread in ovens! These objects can teach us lessons about the entire community.

The citizens of Pompeii bathed in public bathhouses. It is generally believed that the men and women bathed separately. The remains of many of these bathhouses still stand today.

Perhaps the most amazing artifacts found in Pompeii are its pieces of art. The artwork has stunned historians with its beauty. Much of Pompeii's artwork is in the style of fresco. Frescoes are made by painting on fresh, moist plaster. Mosaics were also common in many homes. They were either hung on walls or used for floor decoration. To create mosaics, artists used small pieces of colored tile. These pieces of tile are called tesserae.

Pompeii's paintings have very different styles. Some of them mimic Roman architectural details. For instance, an artist may have painted what appeared to be a three-dimensional column on a flat wall. This kind of artwork tricked viewers into thinking they were seeing an actual column. Many artists also created landscapes. These include gardens, festivals, and paintings of the sea. This artwork shows that the citizens wanted to see nature's beauty, even while relaxing in their own homes.

WARNING

One of the most famous mosaics in Pompeii is a warning. The mosaic was found in the entrance of a home known as the House of the Tragic Poet. The mosaic shows a chained-up, black-and-white dog. The dog is crouched and baring its sharp teeth. Next to the dog are the words *Cave canem*. This Latin phrase means "Beware of the dog"!

Standards of Living

Portraits were also popular in Pompeii. They give archaeologists clear clues about their subjects' way of life. This can be seen in the famous *Portrait of a Husband and Wife*. In this painting, the wife holds a writing tool to her lips. Her husband stands beside her. He holds a paper scroll. These activities let us

Warnings such as this Beware of the Dog sign were made from small pieces of colored tiles. This kind of work is called mosaic.

know the couple is well educated. They are both able to read and write. Historians have observed that in ancient times only wealthy people were educated. Thanks to one simple painting, archaeologists can imagine how rich this couple must have been.

ARTIFACT

Works of art found in Pompeii in the seventeen and eighteen hundreds greatly affected the art of that period. Artists began to re-create wall paintings and copy themes from this newly discovered Roman art.

Between 1894 and 1895, the House of the Vettii was excavated. Artwork inside the house caused a great stir. The bronze artworks, marble statues, and paintings were all in amazing condition. That's because the homeowners were very wealthy. After the earthquake in A.D. 62, they still had money to spare. So they were able to afford the best materials to restore what they had lost.

This is a fresco of a married couple who lived in Pompeii. Historians use this type of artwork to build a clearer picture of what life in Pompeii must have been like.

This human skeleton was dug out of the volcanic mud that covered Herculaneum. Due to this volcanic mud, digging up Herculaneum has been much more difficult than digging up Pompeii.

CHAPTER FOUR

Difficult Digs, Difficult Decisions

The fury of Vesuvius wasn't limited to Pompeii. One of the other nearby ancient Roman cities destroyed by the eruption was Herculaneum.

There was an important difference in what the volcano did to the two towns. While Pompeii was covered with hot ash, Herculaneum was drowned in volcanic mud. This mud quickly set and hardened. Once it did, it was as strong as concrete. Excavations in Herculaneum began in full force in 1738. However, diggers have faced many stops and starts along the way. This is due, in part, to how tough the material is to break through. It means that excavations must proceed more slowly than at Pompeii.

Digging Up Bones

Historians believe unearthing the Herculaneum site is crucial. The site can provide scientists and other experts with a new understanding of ancient Rome.

For example, the nature of human remains being studied in the two buried cities is very different. At Pompeii, people have carefully examined Fiorelli's plaster casts. These casts are extremely helpful to archaeologists. However, there is nothing better than finding and studying ancient bones. In Pompeii, there are no bones to study. The casts are all that is left to study of the victims' bodies.

Them Bones

On the other hand, scientists have found a huge amount of skeletal remains in Herculaneum. This is a very important find because during the Roman Empire people did not bury their dead. Instead, they practiced cremation, or burning a dead body to ashes. Because of this, examples of Roman human remains are rare. The skeletons that are found in Herculaneum are all in similar poses. The poses show that the victims were huddled together in corners, attempting to find shelter, or trying to escape. Clearly, their last moments at Herculaneum were filled with great terror.

Hard Rock

Archaeologists are convinced that excavating Herculaneum is an important goal. They are also convinced that reaching their goal will be extremely difficult. This is partly because the town was buried under 65 feet (19.8 m) of rock-hard mud.

There are other challenges to consider. One of them is that Herculaneum is buried beneath another city! The city on top of Herculaneum is a modern thriving town called Portici. If excavations continue, they will disrupt the lives of people living in this city. Diggers would have to damage the current city to unlock the secrets of the ancient city below. This forces historians to tackle important questions. Do they sacrifice a new town for an old one? Or do they sacrifice learning more about our history?

Balancing Act

Pompeii's future is uncertain. Pollution is slowly damaging the ruins. Also, crowds continue to arrive to see the city. Over two million people flock there each year. They want to witness this connection with ancient Rome. However, their presence may be doing more harm than good. Too many visitors might destroy the site that nature preserved for centuries.

The future of Pompeii's ruins is uncertain. A group called UNESCO is trying to help the balance. UNESCO stands for the United Nations Educational Scientific and Cultural Organization. The group understands that Pompeii needs

This skeleton dug up from the ruins of Herculaneum was found wearing jeweled gold rings on its fingers.

protection. It must be cared for. That is why it declared Pompeii a World Heritage Site.

UNESCO wants to ensure that new generations get to see the ruins. They are working to re-create how Pompeii might have looked before the eruption. For instance, gardens in homes have been replanted. They have been filled with flowers and trees that grew in Pompeii centuries before.

Lessons That Won't End

Both Pompeii and Herculaneum have produced wonderful artifacts. Archaeologists have dug up skeletons, buildings, and priceless artworks. However, the greatest treasure these sites have given is knowledge. Pompeii and Herculaneum are the ruins of entire cities. Their everyday objects, houses, and graffiti all give us incredible snapshots of an era long ago. By studying them, we get a view of what daily life was like in ancient Rome. The sites help us understand a different culture. This is the greatest gift for archaeologists. After all, their work revolves around connecting our lives with those of our ancestors.

New Words

aqueduct (**ak**-wuh-duhkt) a large structure built to carry water across a valley

archaeology (ar-kee-**ol**-uh-jee) the study of the past by digging up old buildings and objects and examining them carefully

artifact (**art**-uh-fakt) objects made by people who lived long ago

decompose (dee-kuhm-**poze**) to rot or decay

excavate (**ek**-skuh-vate) to dig in the earth

extinct (ek-**stingkt**) something that has died out

fragment (**frag**-muhnt) a small piece or a part that is broken off

graffiti (gruh-**fee**-tee) pictures drawn or words written on the walls of buildings or other surfaces

impluvia (im-**pluv**-i-a) a Latin word meaning water tanks

New Words

irrigation (ihr-uh-**ga**-shuhn) a system of supplying water using artificial means

lapilli (la-**pil**-li) fragments of lava ejected in a volcanic eruption

lava (**lah**-vuh) the hot, liquid rock that pours out of a volcano when it erupts

layout (**lay**-out) the pattern or design of something

mosaic (moh-**zay**-ik) a pattern or picture made up of small pieces of colored stone, tile, or glass

ravages (**ra**-vij-iz) violently destructive effect

subject (**suhb**-jikt) a person who lives under the authority of a king or queen

suffocated (**suhf**-uh-kat-ed) having died from lack of oxygen

For Further Reading

Bisel, Sara C. *Secrets of Vesuvius: Exploring the Mysteries of an Ancient Buried City.* New York: Scholastic Inc., 1993.

Caselli, Giovanni. *In Search of Pompeii: Uncovering a Buried Roman City.* Columbus, OH: McGraw-Hill Children's Publishing, 1999.

Howarth, Sarah. *Roman Places.* Brookfield, CT: Millbrook Press, Inc., 1995.

Patent, Dorothy Hinshaw. *Lost City of Pompeii.* Tarrytown, NY: Marshall Cavendish Corp., 2000.

Tanaka, Shelley. *The Buried City of Pompeii: What It Was Like When Vesuvius Exploded.* Collingdale, PA: Diane Publishing Co., 2003.

Resources

Organizations

National Geographic Society
P.O. Box 98199
Washington, D.C. 20090-8199
(800) 647-5463
http://nationalgeographic.com/

World Heritage Centre
UNESCO
7, place de Fontenoy
75352 Paris
France
http://whc.unesco.org/

Web Sites

BBC History—Pompeii: Portents of Disaster
www.bbc.co.uk/history/ancient/romans/pompeii_portents_01.shtml
This informative site explains why the people of

Pompeii were caught off guard by the eruption of Vesuvius. The site also provides a time line of the ancient Roman Empire.

Discovery Channel
http://travel.discovery.com/ideas/culture_attractions/ 101/histcult/6.html
Do you have a burning desire to see the long lost city of Pompeii? This Web site gives you information about how you could take a tour of these amazing Italian ruins!

The History Channel: Pompeii
www.historychannel.com/perl/print_book.pl?ID=107838
An important overview of Pompeii's destruction can be found on this Web site. There is also a link to information about the burying of another city, Herculaneum.

Index

Index

About the Author

Sarah Pitt Kaplan is a native of St. Louis, Missouri. She studied art history in Memphis, Tennessee, where she learned about the ancient artwork of Egypt, Greece, and Rome. She has visited Pompeii and Herculaneum.